THE UGLY BOOK

THE UGLY BOOK

Andrew Davies

ROBSON BOOKS

Produced in 2005 by
PRC Publishing Limited,
The Chrysalis Building,
Bramley Road, London W10 6SP

An imprint of **Chrysalis** Books Group plc

First published in Great Britain in 2005 by
Robson Books
The Chrysalis Building
Bramley Road, London W10 6SP

An imprint of **Chrysalis** Books Group plc

1 2 3 4 5 6 7 8 9

ISBN: 1 86105 856 X

Printed in Malaysia

Introduction

Let's start with a warning. This could get ugly. In fact, it could get *very* ugly. Because assembled in this small book are some of the most repulsive creatures known to man. Hours of painstaking research—without the use of protective equipment—have gone into assembling this gallery of some of nature's least photogenic creatures. Our research has carried us to the depths of the ocean and to the arid plains of Africa in search of what we'd like to call nature's out-and-out walking, crawling and slithering mingers.

But one person's ugly can be another person's cuddly. Take the familiar Bulldog or the Chinese Shar-Pei (over-wrinkly dog). To some people, the Winston Churchill-lookalike Bulldog is one of the ugliest dogs on the planet with, "a face like it was chewing a wasp." Others, such as Ozzy Osbourne's family, adore the breed, even if they do find it difficult to housetrain their dogs. Around the world there are scores of Shar-Pei appreciation societies, people who extol the virtue of the dog that was used as a farm dog in its native China and was driven to near extinction by state taxes and breeding bans. The fact that it has 50% more skin than is necessary, like a too-big sweater that its auntie knitted, doesn't seem to bother these dogs a bit.

THE UGLY BOOK

And why have we ended up with the phrase "coyote ugly"? We spent fruitless hours looking through a stack of coyote photographs to find one of a coyote looking like it had got out of bed the wrong side, but no, they were all beautiful. Not only that, they tended to make things worse by hanging out in some of America and Canada's finest scenery. Finding an ugly picture of a coyote was impossible, so in the end we had to make do with one looking just a little bit nasty—turning ugly, if you like.

Though there are some members of the animal kingdom for which a jury will never give a unanimous verdict of ugsome, there are quite a few that have a fan club membership numbering zero. Take the gruesome angler fish. The angler is one of many despicable, weirdly-shaped fish lurking about in the depths of the oceans that make an encounter with a great white shark seem mildly pleasant. Few fish are capable of looking happy and the angler fish has got solid grumpy bred into it. No wonder fish parents don't hang around to see what their fry turn into.

Of course we couldn't fill the book with wall to wall hideosity. Mixed in with nature's ugliest ducklings are some common or garden animals caught on a bad day, in bad light, with bad hair, or displaying a bad attitude. Pig lovers might have fallen for the cute, trottered movie star from *Babe*, but we've managed to find at least three not-so-little piggies that are never going to make it onto the silver screen. Unless it's via the catering wagon.

THE UGLY BOOK

There's the top-rated TV programme called *What Not To Wear*—and this book could easily be dubbed, *What Not To Roll In*. Because you can't keep animals out of mud, hedges, dirt, dust, swamps and other animals. So we've sprinkled the book with examples of animals not looking their usual selves. Watch out for a dishevelled boar that looks so down on its luck you could imagine it outside a tube station selling *The Big Issue*.

There are a few fatties in here too, and not just animals that have been overfed by owners who think that more food equals more love. Hibernating alpine rodents stick on the pounds in anticipation of spending a great deal of time buried beneath the snowline. Before they finally make it into their extra-large holes for the long winter months ahead, they look like furry sumo wrestlers with an addiction for nuts.

We've also managed to assemble a wide range of hairstyles that make the legendary Flock of Seagulls look (80s band much quoted on *Friends* for having the very worst hairstyles of any rock band ever) seem like a quick snip at the barber shop. Having seen the dreadlocked dogs on page 79 you begin to wonder what the smell would be like after they've rolled around in the park for a couple of hours and retrieved sticks from ponds. The big upside of owning dogs like that would be if you needed your car cleaned on a regular basis. You could wet them, station them a vehicle width apart, then get them to shake their coats vigorously as you drive between them, handily recreating the action of a car wash. If you wanted your tyres scrubbed at the same time, then buy a couple of smaller ones.

Before anyone goes out and contacts their nearest branch of the RSPCA, we're not serious. *The Ugly Book* has a whole host of similarly intriguing animals, none of which were hurt in the compiling of this book. Unless you count their feelings...

Andrew Davies
October 2004

We don't want to be unkind about this—but in life you have to accept that some of us fell out of the ugly tree.

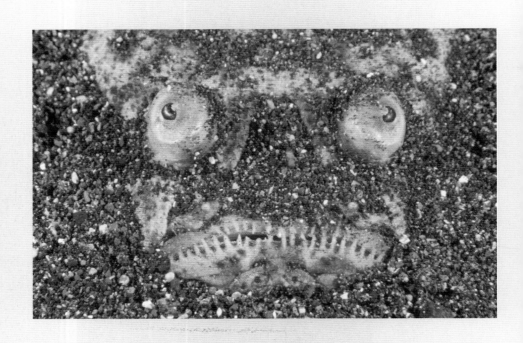

A very tall ugly tree.

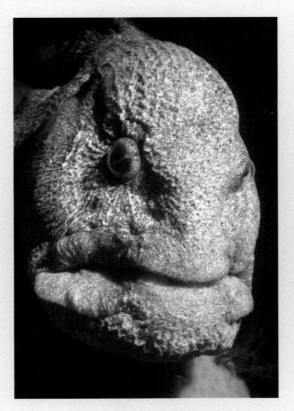

And hit every single branch on the way down…

....And did it on a regular basis.

Call them ugly ducklings.

Complete mingers.

Total munters.

Goppin' ugly, and then some...

Or just good old-fashioned, stomach-churningly repulsive; they have a place in life too.

THE UGLY BOOK

It's just better to avoid them, that's all.

If you suspect you might look too ugsome for even Mingers.com, don't despair.

There's bound to be someone worse off than you.

Whether it's someone nature dealt an unkind blow...

Someone who comes over all slimy...

Or someone wrecked
by a long-term drug dependency.

There are aspects that some cultures find beautiful and others hate. In the Pacific islands it's cool to be fat.

Very fat.

In the West we're not big fans of body hair.

Though bald is rarely beautiful.

And big ears are funny wherever you go.

In life there are different forms of ugly. There's Pug ugly.

Pig ugly.

Coyote ugly.

Butt ugly...

And not forgetting, ugly bugly bugly.

Some people say that beauty is in the eye of the beholder.

But some people have got very stra-a-a-a-nge eyes.

It is also reckoned that the eyes are the windows of the soul.

And if that's true, you have to ask yourself...

What's so darned sca-a-a-a-ry?

Okay, so you're the kind of person that looks at milk and it turns sour. What to do?

You could try cosmetic surgery.
Get the old schnozz taken down a bit.

A nip and a tuck to get rid of some baggy wrinkles.

A touch of collagen here and there
to make your lips oh-so kissable.

Maybe have those over-large ears corrected.

And the face lifted... and lifted... and lifted.

Making yourself attractive can be an immense task.

You can spend years and years getting there.

But you might just surprise yourself.

THE UGLY BOOK

There are many things you can do to beat the raw deal that fate has dealt you from the gene pool.

Make sure you get enough beauty sleep.

Go to the gym and get your body into shape
(any kind of shape).

If you've got no discipline, get a personal trainer
to put you through your paces.

Don't ignore the evidence right in front of your eyes.
Take a good look in the mirror.

Go on, look yourself square in the eye.

That's assuming any mirrors in the house are still in one piece.

Could you dress a little better?

Is all that unsightly facial hair necessary?

Could you floss a bit more often?

Can you do something about those spots?

Because sooner or later you'll be ready to step onto that pedestal!

It's easy to bury your head in the sand and pretend that nothing's wrong.

And that when people shout, "Yo, big nose!"

They're talking about someone else.

It's not you who's got a face like a dropped pie.

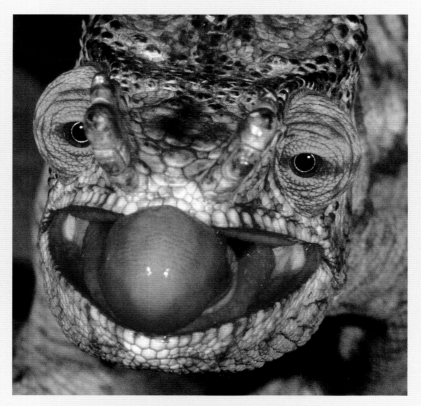

Who could stop all the clocks in a very big clock shop.

Someone gruesome-looking enough to make babies cry.

Remember, skincare is very important.
A mud pack will help soften your delicate epidermis.

It's good for dry skin.

Moist skin...

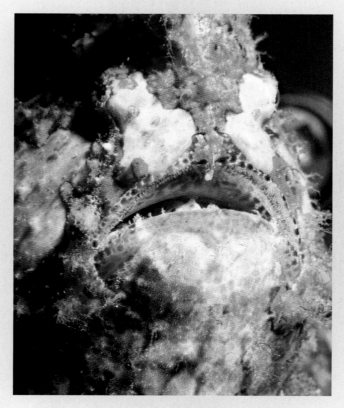

And even nobbly skin.

But whatever you do—don't spend too long in the bathtub.

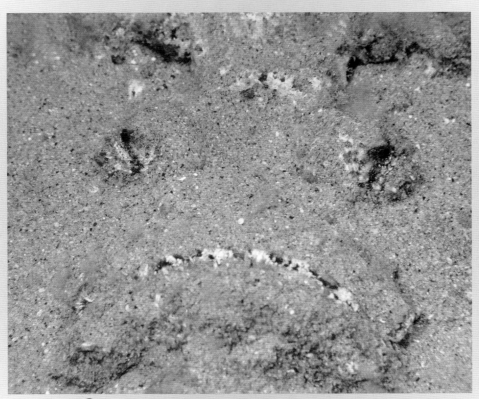

So what do you do if you have a weak chin?

A whiskey drinker's nose...

And breath that could strip paint at five yards.

Apart from sell real estate...

Or car insurance.

You could try getting a makeover. Start with a new hairstyle.

Work out first what suits you best—big hair or small hair.

Celebrity hair maybe? Cher's had enough
to choose from.

Dreadlocks can make a statement, providing
they don't get in the way.

And too big hair will have you tearing photos
out of albums three years down the line

Might we also suggest a pedicure while you're at it.

A new set of frames would be good.

Some new clothes, the dragged-through-the-hedge-
backwards look isn't so hot this year.

But don't mistake "ugly" for "having a bad hair day."

You know the score, when you get out of bed feeling
like a three-headed monster.

When your mouth turns down at the edges.

And the only thing you want to do is hide.

Try smiling! It uses fewer muscles.

Though cackling might be taking things just a little bit too far.

Remember beauty is only skin deep.
Think beautiful and you are beautiful.

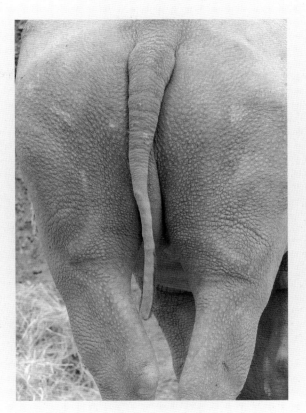

Tell yourself, yes, I have a cute little derriere.

Yes, I have legs to die for.

Yes, I have the mouth of a supermodel.

Tell yourself I am special, I am gorgeous,
I am total, 100% eye candy!

"Come and get me girls!"

Picture Credits